HISTORY IN DEPTH

THE RUSSIAN REVOLUTION

Tamara Pimlott

Poynton County High School, Cheshire

M
MACMILLAN
EDUCATION

First published 1985
Reprinted 1986 (twice), 1987, 1988

Published by
MACMILLAN EDUCATION LTD
Houndmills, Basingstoke, Hampshire RG21 2XS
and London
Companies and representatives
throughout the world

Printed in Hong Kong

British Library Cataloguing in Publication Data
Pimlott, Tamara
The Russian Revolution. — (History in depth)
1. Soviet Union — History — Revolution
1917-1921 2. Soviet Union — Politics and
government — 1917-1936
I. Title II. Series
947.084'1 DK265
ISBN 0-333-36542-9

CONTENTS

Acknowledgements

The author and publishers wish to thank the following who have kindly given permission for the use of copyright material:-

Academic International Press for an extract from *Reign of Rasputin: An Empire's Collapse,* memoir by Michael V. Rodzianko, new introduction by David R. Jones (1973); Gerald Duckworth & Company Ltd. for an extract from *Letters of the Tsar to the Tsaritsa* by N. Romanov; Lawrence & Wishart Ltd. for extracts from *Ten Days that Shook the World* by J. Reed and *Memoirs of Lenin* by N. Krupskaya; Sir Esteban Volkow and the Museo Leon Trotsky for extracts from *History of the Russian Revolution* by L. D. Trotsky.

Every effort has been made to trace all the copyright holders but if any have been inadvertently overlooked the publishers will be pleased to make the necessary arrangements at the first opportunity.

The author and publishers wish to acknowledge the following photograph sources:

BBC Hulton Picture Library pp 5, 9 top, 22, 30, 32, 41, 44; Mansell Collection pp 43; Novosti Press Agency pp 8, 9 bottom, 10, 11, 12, 19, 20, 27, 28, 31, 34, 35, 39, 42, 45; Society for Cultural Relations with the USSR — cover.

The publishers have made every effort to trace the copyright holders, but where they have failed to do so they will be pleased to make the necessary arrangements at the first opportunity.

PREFACE

The study of history is exciting, whether in a good story well told, a mystery solved by the judicious unravelling of clues, or a study of the men, women and children whose fears and ambitions, successes and tragedies make up the collective memory of mankind.

This series aims to reveal this excitement to pupils through a set of topic books on important historical subjects from the Middle Ages to the present day. Each book contains four main elements: a narrative and descriptive text, lively and relevant illustrations, extracts of contemporary evidence, and questions for further thought and work. Involvement in these elements should provide an adventure which will bring the past to life in the imagination of the pupil.

Each book is also designed to develop the knowledge, skills and concepts so essential to a pupil's growth. It provides a wide, varying introduction to the evidence available on each topic. In handling this evidence, pupils will increase their understanding of basic historical concepts such as causation and change, as well as of more advanced ideas such as revolution and democracy. In addition, their use of basic study skills will be complemented by more sophisticated historical skills such as the detection of bias and the formulation of opinion.

The intended audience for the series is pupils of eleven to sixteen years: it is expected that the earlier topics will be introduced in the first three years of secondary school, while the nineteenth and twentieth century topics are directed towards first examinations.

RUSSIA AND THE ROMANOVS

Coronation

On 26 May 1895, Nicholas Alexandrovich Romanov was crowned the fourteenth Romanov Tsar of Russia. Thousands of Russian peasants crowded into Moscow for the celebrations and were treated to free beer, food, dancing and a circus. Unfortunately these festivities went badly wrong. Why, it is not clear; some witnesses said later that there was not enough beer, others that there were not enough mugs. For whatever reason, a stampede occurred and within an hour hundreds of people had been trampled to death. That night Nicholas with his wife Alexandra shocked the population by attending a ball instead of mourning the dead. Superstitious Russians whispered among themselves that the tragedy was a bad omen for the reign of Nicholas II.

Nicholas and Alexandra

As Tsar of Russia, Nicholas ruled as an autocrat, which meant that he had total power and that he could make laws, could appoint and dismiss ministers and could decide whether Russia was to go to war. To maintain this power he increased the number of secret police (Okhrana) who kept watch on the population and who punished those critical of the Tsar.

Who was this man who ruled one of the largest empires in the world? He stood 1.7m tall, a slender man who looked not unlike his English cousin, King George V. The historian, W.B. Lincoln, describes Nicholas' childhood:

Nicholas and Alexandra in traditional Romanov costume

> As a child, Nicholas ate the simplest foods, bathed in cold water, and was even obliged to go hungry on occasion. Heir of a dynasty that possessed vast lands, rich palaces, such priceless treasures as the Great Hermitage art collection and such royal gems as the 195-carat Orlov diamond and the 40-carat Polar Star ruby, he was obliged to sleep on an army cot, with a hard pallet for a mattress. Nonetheless, Nicholas and his younger brothers and sisters, Georgii, Ksenia, Mikhail, and Olga, led perhaps the least disciplined childhood of any Romanovs. Their mother loved fun and gaiety, and allowed them to grow up quite free of that rigid discipline that had been such a part of their predecessors' lives. When guests were not present at lunch or dinner, it was not unusual for the children to dissolve into peals of laughter as they pelted each other with pellets of rolled-up bread.
>
> W.B. Lincoln: *The Romanovs*, 1982

He was educated at home by tutors, the most important of whom was a man called Pobedonostsev. His studies included history, geography and economics and he was also encouraged to become fluent in French, English and German:

> When he was not in the classroom, he lived a carefree life, unconcerned – indeed unacquainted – with the affairs of state to which his father devoted long hours each day. He built snow-houses and went skating with his sister in the winter, gardened and planted saplings in the spring and summer, and chopped wood in the fall. When he grew a bit older, he went out almost every night during the winter social season, enjoying the great array of entertainments to be found in St. Petersburg. He adored the opera, the theatre, and the ballet.
>
> W.B. Lincoln: *The Romanovs*, 1982

At the age of 19 he joined the army for a brief spell. In 1894 he married the German princess, Alix of Hesse, and a year later was crowned Tsar at the age of 26; together they faced the many problems of ruling the Russian Empire.

Russia at the beginning of the twentieth century

Russia was and is a vast country occupying one-sixth of the total land mass of the world. It stretched from the Baltic Sea to the Pacific Ocean

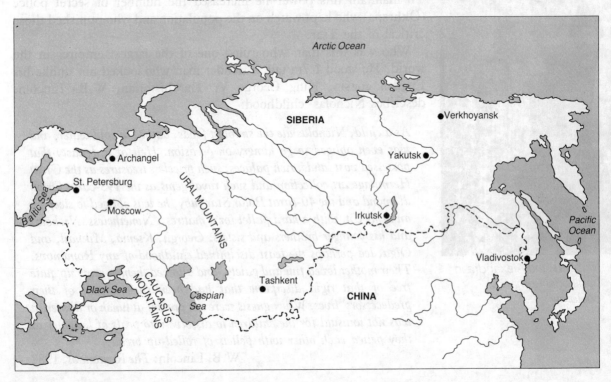

and from the Arctic Ocean to the borders of China and Afghanistan. The area totalled 22 395 000 sq km into which Great Britain would fit nearly 100 times. The distance from north to south was approximately 5 000 km and 9 500 km from west to east. There were large areas where few people could live including central and northern Siberia, the high mountain areas of the Caucasus and the desert regions south of the Caspian Sea. The greatest population density was in the European part of Russia, west of the Ural Mountains. Altogether, 150 different nationalities made up the population of the Russian Empire, ranging from the more sophisticated Russians living in major cities such as Moscow and St Petersburg to the nomadic tribesmen in the southern regions. At the beginning of the twentieth century the population of approximately 140 million could be divided up into the following categories:

Nobles – 1 per cent
The middle class (civil servants, lawyers, doctors and merchants) – 1.5 per cent
Workers living in the towns – 10.5 per cent
Peasants living in the countryside – 87 per cent

Peasants

Although they comprised the largest part of the population, peasants only shared in about 10 per cent of the nation's wealth. An English traveller gave a description of peasant houses at a village near St Petersburg in 1914:

The cottages are built of wood and are unpainted. The entrance is from the side. You mount a wooden staircase or ladder, push open a door and find yourself in the upper or main floor of the cottage, the ground floor being used mainly for storage purposes. A big, whitewashed brick stove is in the middle of the one room; on this stove the older people and children sleep in winter. There is a rough table and a few chairs, a bed and in the middle of the room a child's cot suspended from the ceiling.

Each person consumed only 235 kg of cereals (wheat, rye, barley) a year. In comparison, German peasants ate almost double this amount and French peasants worked land only a quarter of the size of the average Russian plot but produced more from it. Lack of money and education and restrictions placed on them by the village commune (mir) caused much hardship. Diseases such as typhoid, diphtheria and cholera, together with malnutrition, meant that two out of every five children died in infancy.

Scenes from peasant life

Above: *A workers' hostel in Moscow*

Top right: *A typical peasant's hut*

Middle right: *A starving peasant family*

Bottom right: *Peasants weaving baskets*

Lifestyle of the nobility

Right: *A grand Russian tea party*

Below: *A house of the nobility*

Nobles

This extract taken from a book by the Russian nobleman, Tolstoy, describes the start of a typical day for Prince Dmitri Ivanovich Nechlyudov:

The Prince was lying on his high crumpled bed with its springs and down mattress. He had unbuttoned the collar of his fine white linen nightshirt with the well pressed pleats over the chest, and was smoking.... Throwing away the butt of his cigarette ... he put down his smooth white legs, felt for his slippers, threw his silk dressing gown over his broad shoulders and hurried to his dressing-room where the air was filled with perfumes. There, with a special powder, he cleaned his teeth, many of which had gold fillings, rinsed his mouth with scented water and then began to wash his body all over.... He put on clean, freshly ironed linen and boots which shone like glass, and finally seated himself at the dressing table with a brush in each hand to brush his short black curly beard.... He proceeded to the long dining table where three men had laboured the day before to polish the parquetry. The room was furnished with a huge oak sideboard and an equally large table, the legs of which were carved in the shape of a lion's paws. On this table, which was covered with a fine starched cloth with large monograms, stood a coffee pot, a silver sugar bowl, a cream jug with hot cream, and a bread basket filled with freshly baked rolls.

Ornate drawing room in a nobleman's house

Although the nobles comprised the smallest proportion of the population, they controlled 50 per cent of the country's wealth.

Workers

In 1902 the *Moscow Municipal Corporation Report* described rooms in the towns where workers lived:

The apartment was damp and unbelievably dirty. In two rooms there is complete darkness. The ceiling is so low that a tall man cannot stand upright . . . the apartment has a terrible appearance, the plaster is crumbling, there are holes in the walls, stopped up with rags. The stove has collapsed. Legions of cockroaches and bugs. . . It is piercingly cold. Wet clothing and dirty linen; everywhere dampness and dirt. Draughts in every corner; in rainy weather water on the floor two inches deep.

These industrial workers share a corner of one room

Living conditions of metal workers' families in St Petersburg

Conditions were so poor in the factories that four in every 100 workers were seriously injured each year. They were whipped, beaten or fired for the smallest mistake; wages were very low – on an average 200 roubles a year for a family of four, which was not enough to support one man. Strikes were illegal and were savagely suppressed by the Tsar's troops and workers' trade unions were forbidden.

Bloody Sunday and the revolution of 1905

On the 22 January 1905 about 250 000 workers approached the Tsar's Winter Palace in St Petersburg intending to give him a petition explaining the poor conditions in which they worked and lived and appealing to him to improve them. The procession moved peacefully through the snow-covered streets, singing hymns. The workers – women, men and small children – were led by a priest, Father Gapon; as they drew closer to the palace they were faced by a line of motionless Cossack cavalry. With one command from their captain these troops suddenly charged into the crowd weilding their heavy swords and cutting down hundreds of the workers. Bodies littered the ground, their blood staining the snow upon which they lay. Father Gapon (who escaped) later wrote about this dreadful massacre, known as Bloody Sunday:

Horror crept into my mind. The thought flashed through: 'This is the work of our Little Father, the Tsar! There is no longer any Tsar for us!'

Feeding the poor. Industrial workers join the queue for food

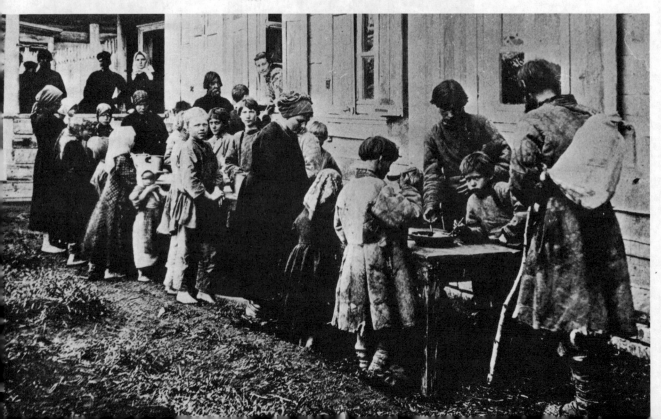

Rebellions and riots by workers, peasants and even sailors (on the battleship Potemkin) broke out throughout the land. There was anger because of the massacre, because of the conditions in which people lived and because of Russia's defeat in the war against Japan in 1904. For a time it seemed that the Tsar would lose his throne. Desperate to keep control, Nicholas issued the *October Manifesto* promising to improve conditions for the peasants and industrial workers; he also agreed to the calling of a Duma (parliament) in which all the classes would be represented. The revolution died down as hopes became centred on the Duma which it was believed would bring new reforms. By 1906, however, the Tsar made it clear that he was unwilling to share any power with the Duma:

To the Emperor of all Russians belongs supreme autocratic power. Submission to his power is commanded by God himself.

Using the evidence: Nicholas and Alexandra, an assessment

We have seen some of the problems of Russia and will now look more closely at the personalities of Nicholas II and Alexandra to consider whether they had the necessary qualities to rule.

Nicholas II

A   When his father died, Nicholas cried and said:

I am not prepared to be a Tsar. I never wanted to become one. I know nothing of the business of ruling. I have no idea of even how to talk to the ministers.

B   The historian Edward Crankshaw says:

Nicholas' formidable father died only 49 years old. He had imagined he had many years before him and he had done next to nothing to prepare the way for an heir he found impossible to take seriously.
     E. Crankshaw: *In the Shadow of the Winter Palace*, 1976

C   An account by a British M.P. in 1896:

The Tsar certainly did not give the impression of either mental or physical vigour. It was hard to realise that this slim, not very tall and decidedly delicate looking stripling was the son of the great giant who could twist tin plates in the hollow of one of his brawny hands. He entered the room, shy, uncertain, indecisive, looked back to get a hint, and altogether went to his place with much awkwardness and shamefacedness.

D   Kerensky, who took over the government on Nicholas' abdication in 1917, said of him:

His mentality and his circumstances kept him wholly out of touch with the people. He heard of the blood and tears of thousands upon thousands only through official documents, in which they were represented as 'measures' taken by the authorities 'in the interest of the peace and safety of the state'. Such reports did not convey to him the pain and suffering of the victims... He was an extremely reserved man ... He was not well educated, but he had some knowledge of human nature. He did not care for anything except his wife, his son, and his daughters.... It was a new experience for him to find himself a plain citizen without the duties or robes of state. Old Madame Naryshkina, the lady-in-waiting, told me that he had said to her: 'How glad I am that I need no longer attend to those tiresome interviews and sign those ever-lasting documents! I shall read, walk, and spend my time with my children'.

A. Kerensky: *Memoirs*, 1966

E   Nicholas kept a diary throughout his life. These extracts were written during the early months of his reign:

December 2nd, 1894. – Count Scheremetieff lunched with us; then, at half past two, in the big ball-room, I gave up dear papa's uniforms to the different regiments of which he was honorary chief. Afterwards we drove out with dear Alix. We dined at eight o'clock, and then played four hands on the piano in our own rooms....
December 4th, Sunday. – After our morning coffee, we went with Alix in the garden for a walk. The morning was fine and clear, 12° of cold. At eleven o'clock we went to mass and then lunched with Xenia, Sandro and Kostia. We drove out, and on our way stopped to see Aunt Eugenie. We had tea and remained alone in our room downstairs until eight o'clock. I had a lot of papers to read which bored me to death, because I would so much like to have more time to give to my beloved little soul, Alix.

F   Edward Crankshaw wrote:

Nicholas seems to have been possessed by two ideas ... he longed to bring prosperity and happiness to the people and be loved by them and he owed it to his forebears to sustain the autocratic principle.

E. Crankshaw: *In the Shadow of the Winter Palace*, 1976

Questions

1 How does Edward Crankshaw (Extract **B**) explain the reasons behind Nicholas' fear (Extract **A**) of becoming Tsar?

2 What impression does Nicholas make on the British Member of Parliament? (Extract **C**)

3 Why, according to Kerensky, was Nicholas an unsuccessful Tsar? (Extract **D**)

4 Would you expect Kerensky to write a favourable or unfavourable account of Nicholas? Give reasons for your answer.

5 Nicholas' own diary shows one weakness that Kerensky refers to. What is it?

6 Crankshaw (Extract **F**) says that Nicholas had two main ideas on the role of a Tsar. What were they? From what you have read in this chapter would you agree?

7 Do these extracts give you any indication of Nicholas' personal strengths?

Alexandra

A Extracts from her letters to Nicholas:

Don't hide things from me. I am strong but listen to me. I suffer over you as a tender, soft-hearted child, who needs guiding. . . . I am convinced that great and beautiful times are coming for your reign and for Russia. We must give a strong country to Baby [their son Alexis] and dare not be weak for his sake. . . . Be firm. . . . How I wish I could pour my will into your veins.

Alexandra: *Letters of the Tsaritsa to the Tsar*, 1923

B These extracts are taken from the memoirs of Princess Radziwell, a lady-in-waiting who had been at the court of Nicholas' mother (the Dowager Empress) and who now attended Alexandra:

I) *The young Empress was at a disadvantage in a ball gown. Her complexion left much to be desired, and she had red arms, red shoulders, and a red face which always gave the impression that she was about to burst into tears. She knew no one, and she did not seem to wish to know anyone; she danced badly, not caring for dancing; and she certainly was not a brilliant conversationalist. Nothing seemed to interest her, nothing aroused her attention. Even with ambassadors, to whom she was supposed to be particularly polite and attentive, she scarcely exchanged two words, and her thoughts seemed far away.*

II) *She knew very well that she was not popular, but attributed the fact to court intrigues and also to the affection which she was aware her mother-in-law had retained and probably would always retain.*

III) *The remembrance of the Dowager Empress, and of her kindness and affability, added to the dissatisfaction, and the Court balls which were such a feature of the St. Petersburg season, to which so many people had year after year been looking forward with impatience and eagerness, became dull and uninteresting.*

C. Radziwell: *Intimate Life of the Last Tsaritsa*, 1931

C   Edward Crankshaw comments that some historians have tried to be more sympathetic towards Alexandra because her only son, Alexis, was born with haemophilia (an incurable disease in which the blood fails to clot) which caused her constant anxiety. However, Crankshaw goes on:

It does not explain why the 22 year old girl from Hesse, plunged suddenly into the midst of the most over-powering court in Europe, instead of taking stock, immediately started nagging her beloved Nicky at his father's death-bed. It does not explain her instant hostility to the family into which she had entered, or her complete failure to perform her duties as Tsaritsa and to go virtually into hiding for the greater part of her life – trying to confine her children and Nicholas himself to a sort of everlasting cosy tea-party at Tsarskoe Selo (their house outside St. Petersburg). She was not a stranger to royal protocol and etiquette; as one of Victoria's favourite grandchildren, she had largely been brought up at Windsor Castle.

E. Crankshaw: *In the Shadow of the Winter Palace*, 1976

Questions
1 What weaknesses in Alexandra's character are shown in all the extracts?
2 Why is the evidence of Princess Radziwell
   a) useful to the historian?
   b) biased?
3 In what ways does Crankshaw agree with Radziwell?
4 Heading: Nicholas II and Alexandra – a judgement.
   Using all the information given, write your own account of the personalities of Nicholas and Alexandra.

2 LENIN

Childhood

In May 1887 a twenty-one-year-old man, called Alexander (Sasha) Ulyanov, was hung for the attempted assassination of Tsar Alexander III, father of the future Nicholas II. On hearing the news, Sasha's young brother, Vladimir, is said to have shouted 'I'll make them pay for this! I swear it!' 'You'll make who pay?' asked a neighbour, Maria Savenko. 'Never mind, I know,' Vladimir replied.

Vladimir Ilyich Ulyanov was born in 1870. Later in his life, better known by his pen-name Lenin, he became one of the leading figures in the Russian Revolution.

While Tsar Nicholas grew up in the Romanov palaces, Vladimir lived in a comfortable wooden house with a large garden and orchard. His father was a school teacher who became a government inspector shortly before his death in 1885. The family enjoyed a good life and the six children were mainly educated by their mother up to the age of nine. Vladimir idolised his eldest brother Sasha, as their sister, Anna, shows in her memoirs:

> He was always imitating Alexander. Whenever Vladimir was asked what he wanted to play, did he wish to go walking, take his Kasha with butter or milk, he never answered directly, but looked first at Alexander, who generally turned aside and kept his brother in suspense. The older children used to make fun of him because of this, but this never prevented Vladimir from answering 'like Sasha'.

The historian David Shub points out that although the Ulyanov family were not very wealthy:

> The family fund included the money left by Lenin's father and his uncle Vasily; the widow's pension of 1 200 rubles a year; a large house and garden in Simbirsk, which was later profitably sold; and part of the Kokushkino estate which Lenin's mother had inherited. The family fund made it possible for Lenin to postpone earning a livelihood until the age of 27, his brother Dmitri until the age of 28. The family was also enabled to undertake several trips abroad – such as the four months Lenin himself spent travelling in 1895, when he was 25. Lenin continued to receive money from his mother, years later, after he had settled abroad.
>
> D. Shub: *Lenin: a biography*, 1966

17

At school, Vladimir was a model pupil. His leaving report read:

Very gifted, always neat and assiduous, Ulyanov was first in all subjects, and upon completing his studies, received a gold medal as the most deserving pupil with regard to his ability, progress and behaviour. Neither in the school, nor outside has a single instance been observed when he has given cause for dissatisfaction. . . .

D. Shub: *Lenin: a biography*, 1966

After Sasha's death, Vladimir went to Kazan University to train as a lawyer. His report from there read:

During his short stay in the university, he was conspicuous for his reticence, lack of attention and even rudeness . . . he gave grounds for suspicion that he was fermenting trouble. He spent a great deal of time conversing with the most suspicious of the students. . . .

D. Shub: *Lenin: a biography*, 1966

Lenin qualified as a lawyer in 1891 and in 1893, one year before Nicholas became Tsar, he became a Socialist and joined the Russian Marxist party.

Socialism against Capitalism

Europe in the nineteenth century was run on Capitalist lines. Capitalism is a doctrine that encourages individuals to compete for power and wealth against each other. In this way, Capitalists believe that production increases and consequently the nation becomes richer.

There were, however, many who argued that a Capitalist society produced a small number of wealthy, powerful individuals at the expense of the majority, who led harsh lives in inadequate housing and in bad working conditions. This opinion was held by people calling themselves Socialists who thought that society should be organised differently and who believed that:

1 the individual should use his talents not for his own promotion and self-interest but for the good of the country or of the community in which he lived
2 there should be no private ownership of land, property, banks, education or industry but that these should be controlled by the community and that profits should be distributed equally.

Amongst the growing number of Socialists was a German thinker and writer called Karl Marx. His ideas were put forward in the *Communist Manifesto* (published in 1848) and *Das Kapital* (published in 1867, 1883 and 1890). Lenin read Marx's writings avidly and became an ardent follower of his cause.

Marxism

Marx believed that the history of humanity is the history of change and that throughout the centuries there have been class struggles. A summary of his ideas is as follows:

1   **The first stage** in human development was when society was based mainly on land and farming. There was little industry and the majority of land belonged to great landowners who controlled the peasants and ruled their lives. This state of affairs eventually led to friction between the classes.

2   **The second stage** was when society moved towards Capitalism with the growth of industry. Although there were still landowners, a new Capitalist group emerged (the bourgeoisie) who controlled production in factories, distribution through railways and money by owning banks. They were able to do this because they suppressed their workers, the proletariat, in the same way as landowners had suppressed their peasants.

3   **The third stage** could only be achieved by revolution. This was the stage of Socialism. Marx urged the proletariat to overthrow the bourgeoisie and set up a Socialist state based on the ideas that have already been mentioned (see page 18).

Graphic representation of the Marxist view of the composition of Russian society

4   Socialism was only the first step towards the ultimate goal which was Communism. This would be an ideal society based on complete equality in which people would work together for the good of the commune or state. Marx did not, however, explain clearly how a Communist society should be organised or how it was to be achieved. This meant that Marxists often quarrelled amongst themselves as to the best way of bringing about Socialism and then Communism.

Lenin: a chronology

1893	Lenin becomes a Marxist joining a small group in St Petersburg.
1895	Contracts pneumonia and subsequently travels through Europe while recuperating. Meets prominent Marxists such as Plekhanov and writes numerous pamphlets to support his ideas.
1895–7	Imprisoned in St Petersburg for his activities.
1897–1900	Sent to a prison camp in Siberia where he marries Nadezhda Krupskaya in 1898.
1900	Leaves Siberia for exile in Europe. Becomes a co-founder of the Marxist newspaper, ISKRA (meaning The Spark), which is printed in Germany but smuggled into Russia.
1902	Publishes a book entitled *What is to be done?*, in which he tells workers that they cannot achieve a revolution by themselves but need the help of a group of dedicated revolutionaries.
1903	Meeting of the exiled Russian Marxists in London. A split takes place dividing them into two groups: the Bolsheviks (meaning majority) led by Lenin and the Mensheviks (meaning minority). The Mensheviks fear that Lenin, by encouraging a small group to lead the revolution, is creating a dictatorship over the working class.
1905	Lenin returns to St Petersburg because of the 1905 revolution. The Tsar regains control.
1906–17	Lenin leaves Russia for exile in Europe, moving constantly as he is often pursued by the secret police.

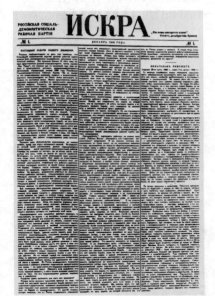

The first issue of Iskra

Using the evidence: Lenin the revolutionary, an assessment
These first extracts describe how Lenin tried to convert town workers to Marxism.

A   Written by Krupskaya:

Vladimir Ilyich was interested in the minutest detail describing the conditions and life of the workers. Most of the intellectuals of those days badly understood the workers. An intellectual would come to a circle and read the workers a kind of lecture... Ilyich read with the workers from Marx's Kapital *and explained it to them. The second half of the studies was devoted to the workers' questions about their work and labour conditions... Gradually other members of our circle also began to use this approach....*

N. Krupskaya: *Memoirs of Lenin*, 1970

B   A fellow revolutionary, Krzhizhanovsky:

His small body, topped by the customary cap, could easily be lost, without attracting attention in any factory district... Dressed in a cloth coat, Vladimir Ilyich could just as easily remain unnoticed in any crowd of Volga peasants... But one had only to peer into the eyes of Vladimir Ilyich, into those unusual, piercing, dark, brown eyes full of inner power and energy, to begin to sense that you were face to face with a far from usual type.

C   Potresov, a Menshevik, recalls his impression on meeting Lenin:

My opinion was that he undoubtedly represented a great force.... His face though was worn; his entire head bald, except for some thin hair at the temples and he had a scanty reddish beard. His squinting eyes peered slyly from under his brows ... he looked like a typical middle-aged tradesman from northern Russia.

D   Krupskaya again:

(I)   *Going the round of the workers' circles, however, could not be done with impunity: police surveillance began to increase. Of all our group Vladimir Ilyich was the best equipped for conspiratorial work. He knew all the through courtyards, and was a skilled hand at giving police-spies the slip. He taught us how to write in books with invisible ink, or by the dot method: how to mark secret signs, and thought out all manner of aliases...*

impunity: free from punishment

aliases: assumed names

(II) *We divided the work up, according to districts. We began to draw up and distribute leaflets... A leaflet was got out for the women workers of the Laferme tobacco factory... They rolled up the leaflets into little tubes so that they could easily be taken one by one and arranged them in their aprons in a suitable manner. Then immediately the hooter sounded, they walked briskly towards the women who were pouring out in throngs from the factory gates and, passing by almost at a trot, scattered the leaflets right into the hands of the perplexed workers.*

N. Krupskaya: *Memoirs of Lenin*, 1970

Questions

1 According to Krupskaya, what methods did Lenin use when speaking to the workers? (Extract **A**)
2 Krzhizhanovsky (Extract **B**) and Potresov (Extract **C**) both give other reasons for Lenin's appeal. What were they and how do they differ from Krupskaya's account?
3 In Extract **D(I)** what problem did Lenin face in talking to the workers?
4 How did he try to overcome this (Extract **D(I)** and **D(II)**)?
5 Write a dialogue between two workers in the Laferme tobacco factory. They have both heard Lenin's speech; one supports him, the other still believes in the Tsar.

Lenin in exile (in Germany and England)

A Krupskaya emphasised Lenin's contribution to Marxism even when Lenin was not living in Russia:

(I) *Vladimir Ilyich gave more and more thought to future work . . . For all practical purposes there was no Party, and no printing press . . . It was necessary to begin with the organisation of an all-Russian newspaper, to establish it abroad, to connect it up as closely as possible with activities in Russia, and to arrange transport in the best way possible. Vladimir Ilyich began to spend sleepless nights. He became terribly thin.*

Lenin's house in London

(II) *Iskra was circulated mainly in double-bottomed trunks taken by Sunday travellers. They took these trunks to various pre-arranged places in Russia, to be called for... The Russian comrades turned the literature out of the trunks and handed it on to the organisation... We corresponded with Iskra agents in Berlin, Paris, Switzerland and Belgium. They helped us in whichever way they were able, finding people willing to take trunks, obtaining money, contacts, addresses and so forth.*

(III) *Lenin spent most of his time writing. I tried to make as little noise as possible as Vladimir Ilyich was then beginning to write What is to be done?.... Afterwards, when we went out for a walk he told me what he was writing and what he was thinking... We used to go for rambles on the outskirts of Munich, choosing the most desolate spots where there were fewer people.*

N. Krupskaya: *Memoirs of Lenin*, 1970

B   This view of Lenin as a Marxist was expressed by Charles Rappaport, a Russo-French Socialist writing in 1914:

We recognised Lenin's achievements. He is a man of iron will and an incomparable organiser of groups. But Lenin regards only himself as a Socialist. Whoever opposes him is forever condemned by him... War is declared on anyone who differs with him... No party could exist under the regime of this Social Democratic Tsar, who regards himself as a super-Marxist, but who is, in reality, nothing but an adventurer of the highest order... I am led to the conviction that Lenin's victory would be the greatest menace to the Russian Revolution. Lenin will hold it in his embrace so tightly he will choke it.

C   J.N. Westwood, historian, writing in 1973:

After release in 1900 Lenin soon went abroad to carry on the struggle for what he considered the correct interpretation of Marxism. He brought to the Socialists a hitherto rare hardness in discussion... He would not compromise, would not admit that his ideological enemies might be partly right. His friends, like Mastov, were only friends so long as their views coincided. And yet, although in politics Lenin seemed devious and unpleasant, there were many who found him an enjoyable companion in private.

J.N. Westwood: *Endurance and Endeavour*, 1973

ideological enemies:
those who did not agree
with his ideas

Questions

1 In what ways does Krupskaya say that Lenin contributed to Marxism whilst in exile? (Extracts **A**(I), (II), (III))

2 To what extent does Rappaport agree with her? What criticisms does he make of Lenin? (Extract **B**)

3 How does Westwood support Rappaport's views?

4 Why do you think Extracts **B** and **C** are more critical of Lenin than Extract **A**?

5 Consider the following instructions that might be given to revolutionaries in exile. Copy out the table. In the second column place the instructions in order of preference according to which you think would be the most useful for your revolutionary party. In the third column, give reasons for your answer.

Instructions	Order of preference	Reasons
Meet with other revolutionaries in exile.		
Keep in touch with events in Russia.		
Give revolutionary speeches.		
Write newspapers and speeches to be smuggled into Russia.		
Live quietly and avoid the police.		
Encourage terrorist activities against the Russian government.		

3

WORLD WAR 1

War!

To add to the problems facing Russia, the country became involved in war:

> *The processions in the streets carrying the Tsar's portrait, framed in the flags of the Allies, the bands everywhere playing the National Anthem ... the long, unending lines of khaki-clad figures who marched away, singing and cheering; tall, bronzed men with honest, open faces, with childlike eyes, and a trusting faith in the Little Father (Nicholas II), and a sure and certain hope that the saints would protect them and bring them back to their villages....*
>
> *Those first days of war! How full we were of enthusiasm, of the conviction that we were fighting in a just and holy cause, for the freedom and betterment of the world! Swept away by the general stir of excitement, we dreamt dreams of triumph and victory! The Russian Steam Roller! The British Navy! The French Guns! The war would be over by Christmas, the Cossacks would ride into Berlin.*

So wrote Meriel Buchanan, the daughter of the British ambassador, in August 1914 when Germany declared war on Russia. In the passage she captures the patriotism and the fervour felt by many Russians together with their whole-hearted support for the Tsar. Yet less than three years later he would be forced to abdicate and, with his family, become a prisoner in Petrograd (St Petersburg was renamed at the outbreak of war because it sounded too German). In this chapter we will follow the slow deterioration of the Tsar's power and the eventual collapse of the Romanov dynasty.

Historians are divided over the question as to whether or not the Tsar was already doomed to fail in 1914. Some say that Nicholas II was in a strong position at this time; he had survived the 1905 revolution, reforms were being carried out to help the peasants and many revolutionaries such as Lenin lived far away from Russia and were still part of minority groups that quarrelled amongst themselves. Russian historians, however, claim that in the cities there was much unrest amongst the workers, with strikes throughout the Empire from 1912 to 1914. They point to the tensions between the Tsar and the Duma, the elected assembly created in 1905. Delegates to the Duma saw themselves as a legislative body, helping the Tsar to formulate laws and rule Russia. He regarded the Duma simply as a consultative assembly and by 1913 was considering its abolition. Above all, Russian historians lend great importance to Lenin's influence in this period, saying that the Bolsheviks were already prepared and poised for revolution.

Why war?

By 1914, Europe was divided into two opposing alliances: Great Britain, France and Russia belonged to the Triple Entente and, on the other side, Germany, Austria-Hungary and Italy formed the Triple Alliance. Tensions had grown up between these important powers and flared into war after the assassination of the Austrian heir to the throne, the Archduke Franz Ferdinand, on 28 June 1914. Amongst the Triple Alliance powers the greatest burden of the fighting fell to Germany, who fought the British and French on the Western Front and the Russians on the Eastern Front.

The Russian army at that time was most impressive; in 1914 it numbered 5 million men, almost double that of France and Germany and four times larger than that of Great Britain. With such numbers it seemed that victory would be certain for Russia. Yet, in December, Meriel Buchanan records:

War! We knew the meaning of it now in all its bitter, cruel truth! There were no cheering crowds about the streets, no flags carried round in procession, no band playing the National Anthem outside the windows. Only silent throngs on the Nevski reading the telegrams posted up on the shop-windows, girls in nurses' dress hurrying to duty, men with grave faces discussing the situation in low voices, women in mourning with dull, heavy eyes, bands of wounded soldiers being taken round and shown the town.

Map of the Eastern Front

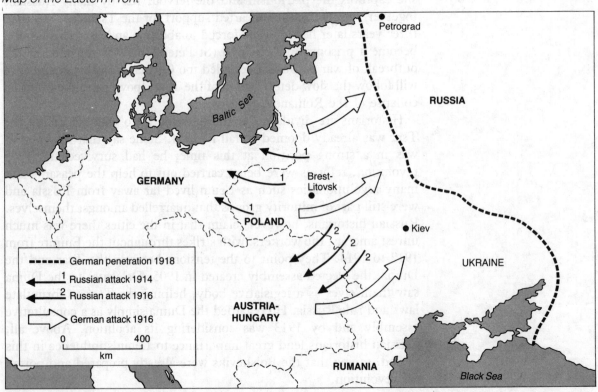

Legend:
- ------ German penetration 1918
- ← 1 Russian attack 1914
- ← 2 Russian attack 1916
- ⇨ German attack 1916

0   400
km

Using the evidence: World War I – why was it a disaster for Russia?

A   The first extracts come from the memoirs of M.V. Rodzianko, President of the Duma:

(I)   *November 1914, Warsaw. Soon after the first battles, shocking reports came from the front of the incompetency of the sanitary department, of its inability to handle the wounded at the front. . . Freight trains came to Moscow filled with wounded, lying on the bare floor, without even straw, in many cases without clothing, poorly bandaged and unfed. . . I went to the Warsaw-Vienna Station where there were about 18 000 men wounded in the battles near Lodz and Berezina. There I saw a frightful scene. On the floor, without even a bedding of straw, in mud and slush, lay innumerable wounded, whose pitiful groans and cries filled the air. 'For God's sake, get them to attend to us. No one has looked after our wounds for five days'. . .*

(II) *General Ruzski had complained to me of lack of ammunition and the poor equipment for the men. There was a lack of ammunition and great shortage of boots. In the Carpathians, the soldiers fought barefooted.*

The Grand Duke (the Commander-in-Chief) stated that he was obliged to stop fighting, temporarily, for lack of ammunition and boots.

A Russian field hospital during World War I

The Empire's Collapse; the memoirs of
M. Rodzianko, 1927

Russian soldiers resting on a captured German aeroplane

B   In December 1916 the War Minister and Russian army commanders held a conference to discuss the difficulties:

(I)   **General Evert:** *We are undersupplied and undernourished ... which reacts banefully on the spirit of the soldiers....*

(II) **General Ruzski:** *We do not receive our meat allowance in the North. The general opinion is that we have everything but it is impossible to get anything. For example, in Petrograd, the poor man is in need but the rich man may have everything. We lack internal organization.*

(III) **General Gurko:** *There is plenty of meat in Siberia but we cannot get it here because we need 300 locomotives which we have not. Our railways are functioning badly, all the railwaymen were sent to the front at the beginning of the war and there is no-one to repair the locomotives.*

(IV) **Rodzianko:** *Members of the Special Council went to examine the cold storage houses near the Baltic Station. They found them in good order; on the outside were mountains of rotting carcasses. On enquiry, it came out that this meat was intended for the army but there was no place to keep it. When permission and money were asked for the new cold storage plants, they were refused. The trouble was that the different Ministries did not co-operate. The supplies department ordered the meat, the railways brought it, but there was no place to store it, and it was not allowed to be placed on the market.*

(V) *Many factories had offered to make more ammunition, but the military authorities refused their offers. Orders were not given to private firms, and the state factories, owing to their poor organization, produced only about one-fifth of what they should.*

C   In August 1915 the Tsar made himself Commander-in-Chief of the Russian army. He left for the front and his letters to his wife reflect the problems that he found there:

(I) *If we should have three days of serious fighting, we might run out of ammunition altogether.*
If we had a rest from fighting for about a month, our condition would greatly improve. It is understood, of course, that what I say is strictly for you only. Please do not say a word of this to anyone.

(II) *Owing to the heat, we take long rides in automobiles and go very little on foot. We selected new districts and explored the surrounding country, being guided by our maps. Often we made mistakes because the maps we have were made eighteen years ago and since then some of the forests have disappeared while new woods and new villages have appeared. . . .*

(III) *Such a great thaw has set in that the positions occupied by our troops where we have moved forward are flooded with water knee deep, so that it is impossible to either sit or lie down in the trenches. The roads are rapidly deteriorating; the artillery and transport are scarcely moving. March, 1916.*

(IV) *The most important and immediate question is fuel and metal, iron and copper for ammunition. Without metals the mills cannot supply a sufficient amount of bullets and bombs. The same is true in regard to railways. Trepov [Minister of Transport] assures me that the railways work better this year than last and produces the proof, but nevertheless, everyone complains that they are not doing as well as they might. July, 1916.*

(V) *Yesterday, although it was Sunday, was a very busy day. At 10 o'clock church; from 11.00 to 12.30, work on the Staff, a big lunch, then Sherbatov's report [Minister of the Interior]; I told him everything. A half-hour's walk in the garden. From 6.00 to 7.30, Polivanov's report in the presence of Alexiev, and after dinner his private report, and then, a mass of beastly papers for signature. . . .*
I . . . would give a great deal to be able to nestle in our comfortable old bed; my field bedstead is so hard and stiff.

*But I must not complain – how many sleep on damp grass
and mud!*

*God bless you, my love, and the children! Tenderly and
passionately I kiss you time without number.*

Ever your old hubby, Nicky. 1916

N. Romanov: *Letters of the Tsar to the Tsaritsa*, 1937

The power of the Empress

Whilst Nicholas was with the army, Alexandra was left to rule
Russia. In 1904, their son Alexis had been born with haemophilia
(see page 16). The slightest cut could be fatal for Alexis as it was
almost impossible to stop the bleeding. Doctors were called in but
they failed to produce a cure and Alexandra turned to spiritual
healers and mystics. One of these, Gregory Rasputin, arrived in St
Petersburg in 1903, styled himself a priest and gained a reputation
for performing miraculous cures. There is controversy over
Rasputin's powers but he certainly helped to ease the young heir's
pains, and in their gratitude the Tsar and Tsaritsa gave him a great
deal of money and made him their closest adviser. He was hated in
the court and throughout Russia because many thought of him as
evil and immoral. Alexandra consulted him during the period that
Nicholas was away and right up until the time of his death, in
December 1916, when he was murdered by a cousin of the Tsar,
Prince Yusupov. During that time there were constant changes in
ministers, some of the oldest and weakest men being brought into
the government. Her letters to Nicholas reflect Rasputin's
influence. She refers to him as 'our Friend':

Rasputin

D   *Forgive me, but I don't like the choice of the Minister of War,
General Polivanov . . . is he not our Friend's enemy?*

Alexandra: *Letters of the Tsaritsa to the Tsar*, 1923

E   In January 1915 the Prime Minister, Kokovtsev, described as
the best financial brain in Russia, was dismissed because
Rasputin did not like him. The 75-year-old Goremykin was put
in his place and he remarked:

*I am like an old fur coat. For many months I have been
packed away in camphor. I am being taken out now merely
for the occasion; when it is passed, I shall be packed away
again until I am wanted next time.*

F   By 1916, food queues were growing in the cities, soldiers were
deserting the army and joining the discontented workers in
groups, known as Soviets, who were committed to over-
throwing the Tsar. The Duma warned Nicholas that the situation
was serious. Rodzianko reported to Nicholas on 20 January
1917:

Queueing for bread in Petrograd in 1917

All Russia is unanimous in claiming a change of Government. . . . To our shame chaos reigns everywhere. There is no Government and no system. . . . At every turn one is confronted with abuses and confusion. . .

        The Empire's Collapse; the memoirs of M. Rodzianko, 1927

G Alexandra wanted to keep the Duma out of government:

Deary, I heard that horrid Rodzianko wants the Duma to be called together – oh please don't, its not their business, they want to discuss things not concerning them . . . they must be kept away.

        Alexandra: *Letters of the Tsaritsa to the Tsar*, 1923

Questions

1 Make a list of all the shortages that the army was facing according to Rodzianko and the generals (**A** and **B**).
2 In what way does the Tsar agree with them? What other problems does he highlight?
3 How did Alexandra make the situation worse? (**D** to **G**).
4 Here is a list of comments that Tsar Nicholas, Alexandra, Krupskaya, a soldier in the army and a member of the Duma may have made in February 1917. Place the comment against the appropriate name:

  a) The Duma is trying to take away your autocratic power. Be suspicious of them and be strong.
  b) What chance do we have of survival against those German guns on the Eastern Front? I am sickened by the stench and death.
  c) At last, our moment has come, our dream will be realised. Russia is weak; we must return to offer an alternative government.
  d) I love my people and have worked so hard for them. Am I to disgrace my family by letting my inheritance now be taken away?
  e) He must go because he is out of touch with what is happening in Russia. If he had been willing to share his power with us, this tragic situation might have been avoided.

The February revolution 1917

In this month strikes escalated in the Russian cities with workers' Soviets occupying factories. Riots broke out as bread queues formed and at the end of February the Duma seized power calling themselves the Provisional Government. A leader, Alexander Kerensky, emerged and on 2 March Nicholas decided that he could not continue to rule as Tsar and issued his abdication:

In agreement with the Imperial Duma, we have thought it well to renounce the Throne of the Russian Empire, and to lay down the supreme power.

Two Russian deserters being attacked by a supporter of the Tsar

Germans guarding a mound of Russian corpses

4

TOWARDS THE NOVEMBER REVOLUTION

Lenin returns

When the February revolution broke out in Russia, Lenin was in Switzerland. Krupskaya wrote: 'From the moment news of the revolution came, Ilyich burned with eagerness to go to Russia.' The problem was – how? Russia's allies, France and Great Britain, wanted Kerensky's Provisional Government to remain in power as they were committed to the war. Lenin had made it clear that he and his Bolshevik supporters would fight for 'bread, peace and freedom'. The Germans realised Lenin's value – if he were to succeed in wresting power from Kerensky, Russia would be pulled out of the war and German troops would be released from the Eastern Front. For this reason, they offered Lenin, Krupskaya and a handful of other exiled Bolsheviks, safe conduct across Germany in a sealed train together with 50 million gold marks. Krupskaya describes that journey:

> In boarding the train, no questions were asked about the baggage and passports. Ilyich kept entirely to himself, his thoughts were in Russia... On arrival in Berlin, our train was shunted on to a siding... On March 31st, we arrived in Sweden... A red flag was hung up in the waiting room and a meeting was held. I remember little of Stockholm; all thoughts were in Russia... From Sweden we crossed to Finland in small Finnish sledges. Everything was already familiar and dear to us ... the wretched 3rd class cars, the Russian soldiers...
>
> N. Krupskaya: *Memoirs of Lenin*, 1970

Arriving at the Finland Station in Petrograd on 3 April 1917, they were greeted by a huge welcoming crowd which had been organised by the Petrograd Bolshevik Party. Krupskaya catches the colour and excitement of that moment:

> The Petrograd masses, workers, soldiers and sailors came to meet their leader... There was a sea of people all around. Those who have not lived through the revolution, cannot imagine its grand, solemn beauty. Red banners, a guard of honour of sailors, searchlights from the Fortress of Peter and Paul illuminating the road ... armoured cars, a chain of working men and women guarding the road... 'Long live the Socialist world revolution!' Ilyich called out to the huge crowd of many thousands surrounding us.
>
> N. Krupskaya: *Memoirs of Lenin*, 1970

33

Many paintings were commissioned after the revolution by the Bolsheviks. This one shows Lenin arriving at the Finland Station in Petrograd. How does the artist make him appear a heroic and popular figure?

Lenin's campaign (*April to November 1917*)

Despite the enthusiasm which greeted Lenin's return, the Bolsheviks were still a minority group. In June 1917, the first All Russian Congress of the Soviets of Workers' and Soldiers' Deputies met. Out of the 1 090 elected delegates, only 105 were Bolsheviks. Most were sailors, soldiers, workers and other revolutionaries, particularly the Mensheviks. It meant that Lenin had to mount a vigorous campaign against the Provisional Government, and to spread the Bolshevik ideas further afield, but he also had to win the support of the Soviets, for without them the Bolsheviks could not hope to seize power. The Party published newspapers which attacked Kerensky's government beginning with comments on Kerensky and his ministers:

Here is a list of their services:
Tseretelli – disarmed the workmen with the assistance of General Polovstsev, checkmated the revolutionary soldiers and approved of capital punishment in the army.
Avksentiev – put several hundred peasants in prison, members of the Land Committees, and suppressed dozens of workers' and soldiers' newspapers.
Nikitin – acted as a vulgar policeman against the railway workers.
Zarvdny – put some of the best workers of the Revolution, soldiers and sailors in prison.
Kerensky – it is better not to say anything about him. The list of his services is too long.

The newspapers carried Lenin's propaganda:

> *The Kerensky government is against the people. He will destroy the country. This paper stands for the people and by the people – the poor classes, workers, soldiers, and peasants. The people can only be saved by the completion of the Revolution and All power to the Soviets – both in the capital and in the provinces.*
> *Immediate truce on all fronts. An honest peace between peoples.*
> *Landlords' estates – without compensation – to the peasants.*
> *Workers' control over industrial production.*
> *A faithfully and honestly elected Constituent Assembly.*

Lenin made speeches in the cities:

> *Stand up against this damned war! This can be done only by a revolutionary Government, which would speak really for the workmen, soldiers and peasants of Russia and would appeal over the heads of the diplomats directly to the German troops, fill the German trenches with proclamations in the German language . . . our airmen would spread these proclamations all over Germany.*

Lenin had to flee to Finland on 6 July (he was to return in October) when the Provisional Government ordered his arrest. He wrote to party leaders in Petrograd and Moscow, urging them to stage a revolution:

> *We must move the loyal regiments to the most strategic points . . . we must occupy the fortress of St. Peter and St. Paul; we must arrest the general staff and the government . . . we must mobilize the armed workers . . . we must occupy the telegraph and telephone stations at once . . .*

The Provisional Government fails

The months from April to October 1917, were a time of great confusion throughout Russia. There were riots and a general breakdown of law and order with peasants seizing land for themselves in the countryside. In the cities, the power of the Soviets grew and there was wide scale desertion from the army, but despite all this the Provisional Government remained committed to the war.

In August 1917, during the confusion, General Kornilov, Supreme Commander of all the Russian armies, threatened to seize power in Petrograd. Kerensky, frightened that Kornilov would succeed, ordered his arrest, and gave ammunition to the Petrograd Soviet (who called themselves the Red Guards) in case Kornilov's troops continued the uprising without him. The Bolsheviks realised that about 25 000 men would be armed with machine guns and rifles and Lenin urged that the time had come for revolution.

These two photographs were taken in 1917 and show how clever Lenin was at disguise

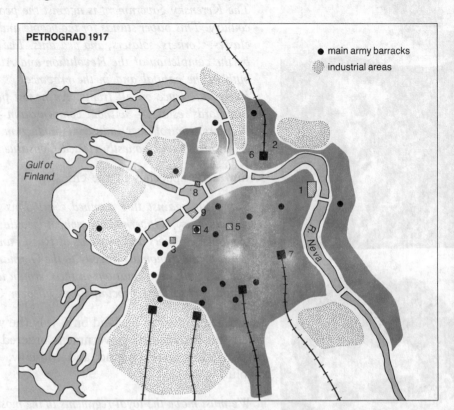

Key to map:
1 Smolny Institute (a famous school which in November 1917 became the Bolshevik headquarters)
2 Vyborg District
3 Central Post Office
4 Telegraph Office
5 State Bank
6 Finland Station
7 Moscow Station
8 St Peter and St Paul Fortress (built in 1703 to protect the city)
9 Winter Palace (the Tsar's palace)

Descriptions of the preparations leading up to the seizure of power in Petrograd on 7 November 1917 came from Leonid Trotsky, one of Lenin's ablest supporters, John Reed, an American journalist living in Petrograd, and Kerensky himself.

A Trotsky, from the Bolshevik headquarters in the Smolny Institute, describes preparations for the November revolution:

The twelfth hour of the revolution was near. The Smolny was being transformed into a fortress. In its garret there were a dozen or two machine guns. . .

November 6, a grey morning, early. I roamed about the building from one floor to another . . . to make sure that everything was in order and to encourage those who needed it. Along the stone floors of the interminable and still half-dark corridors of the Smolny, the soldiers were dragging their machine guns. . .

On the third floor of the Smolny, in a small corner room, the Committee was in continuous session. All the reports about the movement of troops, the attitude of soldiers and workers, the agitation in the barracks . . . the happenings in the Winter Palace – all these came to this centre.

All that week I had hardly stepped out of the Smolny; I spent the nights on a leather couch without undressing, sleeping in snatches, and constantly being roused by couriers, scouts, messenger-cyclists, telegraphists, and ceaseless telephone calls.

L.D. Trotsky: *History of the Russian Revolution*, 1965 ed.

B John Reed describes Petrograd just before the revolution:

Petrograd presented a curious spectacle in those days. In the factories the committee-rooms were filled with stacks of rifles, couriers came and went, the Red Guards drilled... In all the barracks meetings every night, and all day long interminable hot arguments... Hold-ups increased to such an extent that it was dangerous to walk down side streets... One afternoon I saw a crowd of several hundred people beat and trample to death a soldier caught stealing...

At Smolny, there were strict guards at the door and outer gates demanding everybody's pass. The committee rooms buzzed and hummed all day and all night, hundreds of soldiers and workmen slept on the floor, wherever they could find room...

Gambling clubs functioned hectically from dusk to dawn, with champagne flowing and stakes of 20 000 roubles. In the centre of the city at night prostitutes in jewels and expensive furs walked up and down the crowded cafes. Monarchist plots, German spies, smugglers hatching schemes...

And in the rain, the bitter chill, the great throbbing city under grey skies rushing faster and faster towards – what?

J. Reed: *Ten days that Shook the World*, 1966

C On the day of 7 November Trotsky describes the take-over of key points in the city:

On the 7th, there was difficulty at the telephone exchange. Military students had entrenched themselves there, and under their protection the telephone operators went into opposition to the Soviet and refused to make our connection... The Military Revolutionary Committee sent a detachment of sailors to the Telephone Exchange, and the detachment placed two small guns at the entrance... The telephone girls ... fled with hysterical screams through the gates... The sailors managed somehow to handle the work of the switchboard. Thus began the taking over of the organs of administration.

Almost simultaneously with the seizure of the Telephone Exchange a detachment of sailors from the Marine Guard, about forty strong, seized the building of the State Bank...

The citizen slept in peace, ignorant of the change from one power to another. Railway stations . . . have been occupied. . .

At the railway terminals, specially appointed Commissaries are watching the incoming and outgoing trains, and in particular the movement of troops.

Peter and Paul Fortress . . . is today completely taken possession of. . . Machine guns are set up on the fortress wall to command the quay and bridge.

L.D. Trotsky: *History of the Russian Revolution*, 1965 ed.

D   Kerensky tried to maintain power but without success. In his memoirs he later wrote:

At the headquarters of the Petrograd Military District . . . the night of November 6–7 was a time of tense expectation. We were waiting for troops to arrive from the front. They had been summoned by me in good time and were due in Petrograd on the morning of November 7. But instead of the troops, all we got were telegrams and telephone messages saying that the railways were being sabotaged. . .

The hours of the night dragged on painfully. From everywhere we expected reinforcements, but none appeared. There were endless telephone negotiations with the Cossack regiments. Under various excuses, the Cossacks stubbornly stuck to their barracks, asserting all the time that 'everything would be cleared up' within fifteen or twenty minutes and that they would then 'begin to saddle their horses'. . . Meanwhile the night hours passed. . . Not a word from the Cossacks. . .

A. Kerensky: *Memoirs*, 1966

E   The sailors joined in the revolution sailing some of the ships, including the cruiser *Aurora*, up the River Neva to Petrograd.

Finally, the Winter Palace was seized and the government surrendered. Trotsky gives an account of this:

The Ministers, who had sought refuge in the Winter Palace . . . were guarded only by a company of the Women's Battalion and a few of the cadets from the Military Schools. At six in the evening a message was sent into them calling on them to surrender immediately, but as no answer was received the attack on the Palace was opened by a few blank rounds being fired from the Fortress as a preliminary warning. This was followed by a massed onslaught from all sides, armoured cars and machine guns firing at the Palace from under the archway on the square, while now and then the guns of the Fortress or of the cruiser Aurora thundered and crashed above the general din. Actually, however, a

The Winter Palace after the revolution

good many of the shots were only gun-cotton, and the firing in all cases was so inaccurate that the Palace was only hit three times from the river, though on the other side the walls were riddled with innumerable bullet marks, and a good many of the windows were broken.

At the [British] Embassy the noise was almost deafening, though from the windows we could only see the occasional red spit of a gun flashing in the darkness, and at about two in the morning the firing ceased and a little later a shouting cheering rabble of soldiers surged across the bridge.

Both the women soldiers and the cadets had put up a brave defence, but they were greatly outnumbered and when the Bolsheviks gained an entrance . . . the Ministers, gathered in one of the inner rooms, knew that their only hope lay in surrender.

L.D. Trotsky: *History of the Russian Revolution*, 1965 ed.

F   Kerensky fled from the city in dramatic circumstances:

We entered by car. . . . Finally we moved. We followed closely all the details of my daily travel through the city. I occupied my usual seat – on the right in the rear. I wore my customary semi-military uniform, which had become so familiar to the population and to the troops. . . I need hardly say that the entire street – pedestrians and soldiers – recognised me immediately. The soldiers straightened up, as they would ordinarily have done. I saluted, as usual. In all probability, the moment after I passed not one of them could account to himself how it was possible for him not only to have permitted this 'counter-revolutionist', this 'enemy of the people' to pass, but also to have saluted him.

Having passed safely through the centre of the city, on entering the workmen's section and approaching the

Moscow Toll Gate we increased our pace and, finally, moved with breakneck speed. I remember how at the very exit from the city, Red Guardsmen, patrolling the road, came rushing towards our machine from all sides . . . but we had already passed them, while they had not only failed to make an effort to stop us, but had not even had time to take a good look at us.

A. Kerensky: *Memoirs*, 1966

G By 8 November pamphlets and posters issued by Lenin proclaimed:

To the Citizens of Russia! The Provisional Government is overthrown. State power has passed into the hands of the organ of the Petrograd Soviet of Workers' and Soldiers' Deputies, the Military Revolutionary Committee, which stands at the head of the Petrograd proletariat and garrison. The cause for which the people have fought – the immediate proposal of a democratic peace, the abolition of landlords' claims to the land, workers' control of production, the creation of a Government of the Soviets – that cause has triumphed. Long live the Revolution of Workers, Soldiers and Peasants!

H Trotsky's accounts show only the smoothness of the whole operation, John Reed's the bloodshed and the uneasy opposition.

On 10 November Reed walked through the Smolny Institute:

(I) *Inside the long, gloomy halls and bleak rooms seemed deserted. No one moved in all the enormous pile. A deep, uneasy sound came to my ears, and looking around, I noticed that everywhere on the floor, along the walls, men were sleeping. Rough, dirty men, workers and soldiers, spattered and caked with mud, sprawled alone or in heaps, in the careless attitudes of death. Some wore ragged bandages marked with blood. Guns and cartridge-belts were scattered about . . .*

(II) 16 November:
I watched 2 000 Red Guards swing down the Zagorodny Prospekt behind a military band . . . with blood-red flags over the dark ranks of workmen, to welcome home again their brothers who had defended 'Red Petrograd'. In the bitter dusk they tramped, men and women, their tall bayonets swaying; through streets faintly lighted and slippery with mud, between silent crowds of bourgeois, contemptuous but fearful. . . So many were against them – business men, speculators, investors, landowners, army officers, politicians, teachers, students, professional men,

shopkeepers, clerks and agents. The Mensheviks hated the Bolsheviks with an implacable hatred. On the side of the Soviets were the rank and file of the workers, the sailors, all the undemoralized soldiers, the landless peasants and a few – a very few – intellectuals.

J. Reed: *Ten Days that Shook the World*, 1966

Questions

1 The following chart gives some reasons for the success of the overthrow of the Provisional Government. Copy out the table and fill in your answers.

Reason	Order of preference	Further details and comments
Incompetent rule of the Provisional Government		
Effects of the war		
Growing power of the Soviets		
Peasants were discontented		
Leadership of Lenin		
Government lost support of the army		

The Tsar, surrounded by guards, after his abdication. Note how haggard his face looks here compared to the photograph of him on page 5

2 Here is a list of comments that Kerensky, Lenin, a foreign journalist and a landowner may have made on 9 November 1917. Place the comment against the appropriate name.
   a) The Revolution has been won in Petrograd alone. In the rest of Russia there is still much to be done.
   b) I fear for my life and property. This government is committed to nationalisation of land.
   c) Had reinforcements arrived, the revolution would have been lost.
   d) Confusion and suspicion are everywhere in this blood-stained city.

3 Write down the comments that may have been made by: a peasant; a businessman; a Menshevik; the German Kaiser; the ex-Tsar.

5

THE STRUGGLE FOR SURVIVAL 1917-24

The Bolsheviks take control

The Provisional Government in Petrograd had been overthrown by Bolsheviks, Mensheviks, other groups such as the Social Revolutionary Party (SRP), workers, soldiers and sailors, some of whom belonged to one of these parties and others who did not belong to any.

Many dramatic posters such as this were produced after November 1917. This one is dedicated to the sailors who helped in the revolution

A poster showing the worker smashing the old order

Lenin was now determined that the Bolsheviks should emerge as the controlling party and he therefore took the following measures:

1   He formed a government of 15 Bolsheviks known as the Council of People's Commissars with himself as chairman and the Bolshevik Party was renamed the Communist Party.
2   The Provisional Government had called an election to the Constituent Assembly. This was allowed to continue but as less than half the members elected were Bolsheviks, the Red Guards closed the Assembly after only one day.
3   A series of decrees banned all newspapers except Communist ones. The Tsar's Okhrana became known as the Cheka and executed over 50 000 people in 1918. Other decrees allowed peasants to seize the nobles' land even though Communists were committed to nationalisation. Lenin hoped that this measure would bring peasant support for the party.

4 The government took control of banks, industry and transport. It confiscated the land and wealth of the Russian Orthodox Church and abolished all titles except that of 'comrade' or 'citizen'.

5 In March 1918 the Treaty of Brest Litovsk ended the war with Germany. As a result of this treaty, Russia lost valuable land such as the grain growing region of the Ukraine, about a third of her population and half of her industrial areas.

Civil war 1918–22

After 1918 opposition to the Communists arose from many quarters, including the Mensheviks, the Tsar's supporters and Britain and France who felt that Lenin had deserted them during the war. As a result, civil war broke out between the Communist supporters, who banded together in the Red Army, and their opposers, in the White Army. It was a time of great bloodshed and atrocities were committed by both sides. Trotsky was made Commissar of War and through his efforts the Red Army grew from an ill-assorted band of men to an efficient fighting force. By 1922 the Communists had established themselves in total control of the country but the price they had paid was high.

In 1918 Lenin had been shot by Fanya Kaplan, an SRP member; he survived but never recovered full health. The Tsar and his family disappeared, supposedly executed by the Cheka in July 1918. Russia

Children starving during the civil war

was in chaos; there was widespread starvation and industry was so run down that production levels were below those of Nicholas' reign. Typhus, cholera and malaria swept the country. In an effort to restore order, Lenin introduced his New Economic Policy (N.E.P.) allowing peasants to retain their land and sell off their surplus; he allowed a proportion of industry to return to private ownership and encouraged foreigners to come to Russia to set up as investors and financial experts. Lenin said that he needed a breathing space, a time before a real Socialist state could be set up – but time, for Lenin, was running out.

Lenin's death

At 8 p.m. on 21 January 1924 it was announced in Moscow that comrade Lenin had died two hours earlier of a massive brain haemorrhage. Arthur Ransome, a British journalist living in Moscow at the time, recalled the reaction to Lenin's death:

> *When Congress met at 11:00 this morning, Kalinin was hardly able to speak and announced Lenin's death in a few broken sentences. Almost everybody in the great theatre burst into tears and from all parts came the hysterical wailing of women. Tears were running down all faces ... even the funeral march of the Revolutionaries was played by a weeping orchestra.*

Lenin lay in state for four days in the Hall of Columns in Moscow and thousands queued in icy conditions to pay their respects to him in his open coffin. A temporary wooden mausoleum was erected in Red Square next to the Kremlin wall, a position given only to the heroes of Russia. After his funeral Lenin was placed inside it but his body was removed shortly afterwards. His organs and body fluids were removed and special preservatives were applied to his body as part of an embalming process, after which he was dressed in a suit, shirt and tie,

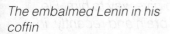
The embalmed Lenin in his coffin

laid in a sealed glass coffin with his head resting on a white pillow and placed in a specially constructed mausoleum.

There was much controversy as to whether or not it really was Lenin's body or a wax effigy in the coffin. Due to this existing doubt, journalists from all over the world were invited to Moscow in the 1930s to witness the embalming chemist opening the coffin and tweaking Lenin's nose and turning his head from side to side, which convinced those present that they were indeed gazing at Lenin's mortal remains.

Today, Communists from all over the world and millions of Russian people still visit the heavily guarded stone mausoleum to pay their respects to Vladimir Ilyich Ulyanov.

Using the evidence: Lenin's achievements, an assessment

A   Stalin, Lenin's successor in 1924:

> *For 25 years Comrade Lenin moulded our Party and finally trained it to be the strongest and most highly steeled Workers' Party in the world . . .*
>
> *Ours is the only country where the crushed and labouring masses have succeeded in throwing off the rule of the landlords and capitalists and replacing it by the rule of workers and peasants. . . . The greatness of Lenin lies above all in this, that by creating the Republic of Soviets he gave a practical demonstration to the oppressed masses of the world that the rule of landlords and capitalists is short lived. . . . He thus fired the hearts of the workers and peasants of the whole world with the hope of liberation.*

B   V. Serge, a fellow revolutionary, describing Lenin in 1920:

> *In the Kremlin he still occupied a small apartment built for a palace servant. In the recent winter he, like everyone else, had no heating. When he went to the barber's he took his turn, thinking it unseemly for anyone to give way to him. He knew that he was the Party's foremost brain and recently, in a grave situation, had no worse threat than that of resigning from the Central Committee . . .*

C   *This extraordinary figure was first and foremost a professional revolutionary. He had no other occupation . . . A man of iron will and inflexible ambition he had no scruple about means and treated human beings as mere material for his purpose. Short and sturdy, with a bald head, small beard and deep-set eyes, Lenin looked like a small tradesman. When he spoke at meetings his ill-fitting suit, his crooked tie, his general nondescript appearance disposed the crowd in his favour. 'He is not one of the gentlefolk, he is one of us,'* they would say. This is not the place to describe in detail the terrible achievements of Bolshevism – the shameful peace with Germany, the plundering of the educated and propertied classes, the long continued terror with its thousands of innocent victims . . . Never in modern times has any great country passed through such convulsion . . .

Both the Communist Party and the Council of People's Commissaries were completely under Lenin's control. It happened sometimes that after listening to a discussion of two conflicting motions in some meeting under his chairmanship, Lenin would dictate to the secretary, without troubling to argue the point, some third resolution entirely his own.

The Communist experiment brought Russia to economic ruin, famine, and barbarism.

The Times, 23 January 1924

D The state he brought into being proved to be more unjust and tyrannical than the state he overthrew . . . The Cheka was only the Tsarist Okhrana under another name, more unpitying, more terrifying . . .

The autocracy remained autocratic. The autocrat told the philosophers what to think, the poets what to write, the artists what to paint and the workmen when and how to work; and they all obeyed him because he had the power to enforce obedience. That the autocrat should then believe that he was conferring benefits on the human race is the final irony.

Robert Payne: *The Life and Death of Lenin*, 1964

Questions
1 According to Stalin, what were Lenin's greatest achievements?
2 What kind of a picture is painted of Lenin, the man, by the second extract?
   How does this differ from the view given towards the end of Extract **C**?
3 Robert Payne (Extract **D**) claims that the Communist regime was no better than that of the Tsar. What evidence does he give to support this view?
4 Why do you think that the Russian writers express different views from those of the English writers?
5 Considering these extracts and the information given in this chapter, which of the following statements do you agree with?
   a) The Russian people had suffered greatly but had achieved little by 1924 *or*
   b) The Russian people had suffered greatly but had achieved a great deal by 1924.
   Give reasons for your answer.

INDEX

Numbers in **bold** denote illustrations